Animals That Stand In Dreams

HARLEY ELLIOTT

Hanging Loose Press

Thanks to many poets and editors for their encouragement.
Some of these poems were first published in: THE ARK
RIVER REVIEW, CAROLINA QUARTERLY, EPOS, THE
FALCON, HANGING LOOSE, HIRAM POETRY REVIEW,
NEW: AMERICAN & CANADIAN POETRY, THE NEW
NEWSPAPER, NORTHEAST, THE PENNY DREADFUL,
ROAD APPLE REVIEW, SCHIST, SECOND COMING, THE
SHORE REVIEW, SOUTH, WHITE ELEPHANT, WISCON-
SIN REVIEW, and WORMWOOD REVIEW.

Designed by Harley Elliott

Library of Congress Cataloging in Publication Data

Elliott, Harley.
     Animals That Stand In Dreams

I. Title.

PS3555.L584A85   811'.5'4   76-49917
ISBN 0-914610-08-2

CONTENTS

Hanging Loose Press wishes to thank the National Endowment for the Arts, and the New York State Council on the Arts, for grants in support of this project.

Produced at The Print Center , Inc., Box 1050, Brooklyn, N.Y. 11202, a non-profit printing facility for literary and arts-related publications. Funded by The New York State Council on the Arts and The National Endowment for the Arts.

animus
anima
animal

****

this is for Dave

ALL YOUR FRIENDS

Your friend the crow
was here today
black seed
on an azure field.

Your friends the snake
and the badger with a bloody face
they were here.
Their eyes were dark stars
and they waited on the distant
edge of things.

Your friend the deer
was here today
with antlers piercing the sky
a buckskin that drifted
wind over sand.

Your friends the coyote
and buffalo were here.
Grass grew from their tails.
The teeth of one were luminous.
The horns of the other
like handles for a skull.

All your friends
were here today
moving in their dream skins.
They didn't make a sound.
Their mouths were closed.

A cloud of breath
rose where they stood.
All your friends were here
waiting for you
to find your way.

THE OWL

At night the snowy owl
appears

    his plumage drifts
    and shines about him

on buildings where he stands

opening his wings.

His mouth gleams like china.

There are three men—
one curled in his breast
one in each wing.

His eyes are white roses

that open and close.

FINDING THE BUFFALO

After the sea of curly humps
after the cairns of historical skulls
raised on the dry land

after the last bone
died in your machines

the brown bucolic eye of the buffalo
remained   floating blind
in the caves of the earth.

We are massing
on the underside of light
beyond the sweat and flies
wagonloads of hump   uprooted tongue

the last skins dry in dark museums.

Lose your eyes
and you see us   all the night herds
dark blue beasts

woolly canyons of buffalo running
certain as the midnight
blood that holds you back.

We are the moving forest
the divine thunder

heading straight for your skull.

THE BLACK HORSE

A man called
The Colonel

at a large table
sang a song called
   The Black Horse

his hand
darting
adjusting
the coffee cup
turning the saucer
 In the polished
face of the table
he sees a map of
his early country

and the black horse
riderless
fierce upon the land
a long time ago.

THE JACKRABBIT

The jackrabbits ears are two narrow wings
so ash-gray and pink
that in his hour
    (at the moment of dawn)

they quietly disappear.

The mouth
is a mirage upon his face
dancing through cornfields
    vertical lip cleft
like a man
standing on a far horizon.

The jackrabbits voice
is the blue of open nerves
and is brought forth only
by the forceful intrusion
of some alien thing

and when it does then appear
it will sing in farewell

a very elemental song
concerning the beauty
of all living things.

The eyes of the jackrabbit
    closing
are like two children
asleep
between stones.

THE SNOW LEOPARD

Behind my own eyes
I see snow falling

half asleep in a soft
kansas storm   dreaming the
cloudy snow leopard

awake in the
heavy stars of falling
himalayan snow

Silence in the fields
behind the house and his
cold valley alike

as our breathing
alternates   from rock
to quiet room

slowly I am falling
in love   in sleep
with the leopard of snow

our eyes close from
skull to skull   the snow
falls away

we rise   we leap
in to each other.

DOGS

Stars turn to dogs and fall on Lima, Peru
he explained
and tonight the sky was clear
in the city of numberless dogs.

The sweating glass of beer
shone yellow in the moonlight
and he began to speak
on governments and hunger
while the city slept unaware

outside the courtyard
we could hear
soft running at each word
the dogs,
their noses testing the cold wall,

speaking to each other
like soldiers in the night.

LIZARDS

Asleep I bloom with lizards
every one I ever touched
returns   emerging from my body
as if to remind me of
the life they led
before I entered it.
From all stations on
the axis of the body   they appear
cleaving upward through the skin
like iridescent arrows.
Horned toads blossom
at my hairline
and glass snakes flow
one from each ear.
Twin swifts glide through
my nostrils   the cobalt sides
and brittle blue
light of their eyes
gleaming in the dark. I am
a vault of lizards.
Their nails
click against my teeth
as they arrive   green
and turquoise phantoms.

My wife touches my arm
and it is alien   her touch
her fingers do not
belong   they are so cold
and soft and valueless
among these landscapes of
armor and horn

and when I open my eyes
I am left alone with
what remains:
      patterns of scales
fading in the darkness

     a thin line down
the center of my body
     newly healed
      and cold as ice.

DEAD IN THE FIELDS

Whiteface heifer
dead in the goldenrod
overstuffed
and impersonal as plaster

(just a glimpse
 as we rattle past)
its eyes
two cold suns
in the middle of july.

The roan mare
struck once by lightning
also lay swollen
legs locked straight out

surrounded by hoofprints
of the curious herd.

From her open mouth
a blood covered turtle
blinking golden eyes
in the terrible light

crawling past her teeth
off into the weeds to sleep.

SHARKS

A signal in the field of shark teeth
I return to heavy with fossils

   becomes you
sunbathing on this dead ocean floor
   your soft brown stomach glowing
   like a target in the rocks

   and I feel more than ever as
I near   the cold-blooded grace
   washing over me
     the power in my spine of moving
in this heat the way a heavy fish
might roll in water.

   It is as if you are waiting there
   below me   belly up with black rimmed eyes
and teeth as savage
as the ones you lie upon

while plants are barely growing all around us
   in the undulating light
     and transparent sharks
   turn slowly in the sky.

SLEEPING OUT WITH FLIES

What should be the glorious
night under stars
constellations of teenage girls
dancing in my eyes

explodes into a freak show of flies.
The vibrating word has gone out
up and down the river bank
***Big Piece Of Dreamy Meat
Beneath The Solitary Cottonwood***

and flies are lifting off
following my bright electric headline.
The long legged fly
and thick headed fly

the spear winged fly
stalk eyed fly   stilt legged fly
covering my cheeks
with iridescent beard.

O midnight   I'm suddenly
dancing on the earth
(my sleeping bag
like a large quilted butterfly
flies away upriver)

dancing in my skin of
picture winged fly   big headed fly
flat footed fly
small headed fly
tangle veined fly

and off to one side
the hump backed fly
sings a reedy welcoming song.
I dance across the sky

stars streaking down
into a million rainbow eyes.

THE WINGED DOG

Rampant on a field of falling stars
the flying dog walks the treetops
walks the white
porch railing.

Deep wings half raised
his eyes in the night
are holes of blue sky
blue sky with rain clouds

twin rain clouds
in each eye.

He enters unfortunate faces
the fallen
thighs of prostitutes
the sleep of dying tapdancers

wings spread above
convulsing children
his teeth open
a path in their fear.

The winged dog shimmering
at the bedsides of the poor.

HAWKS

All the hawks are leaving.
They flash by me
in descending lines
   kestrel, coopers, sharp-shinned,
peregrine falcons
dark and intent.
   I am dressed in black
seated, hands palm up
on the too green grass
as they land

   becoming old friends
I had nearly forgotten, dressed in black
we solemnly shake hands.
They are going on a journey

the bladed wings opening as I
take my hands away, aware of
my meat and heaviness and beyond that
the long thin bone that
runs inside each leg
(their tapered claws
 fold together as they rise)

   and the precise number
of hawks I brought to earth,
the long slender wings like two slack
parentheses, shaping the breast,
so unlike these
who have looked at me for a moment
and then turned

their faces narrow and feathered
as they leave.

THE SNAKE

To the first person the snake
was a muscle sleeping on a rock.

To the second person
a flash of brown fire.

The third person saw a room
filled with black diamonds

the fourth saw a magical root
covered with crescents and stars.

To the fifth it sang
a song about murmuring stones

the sixth saw it dance
like earth-colored water
over the fields.

For the seventh it filled
the sky with teeth.

The eighth person saw the face
of a child with serpentine eyes

to the ninth it was a dark rainbow
fallen from the sky.

The tenth felt its skull
growing deep in his own
its ribs springing like flowers
down the length of his spine.

TWO COYOTES

1

My sleep is touched
with the corpses
of coyotes
     scalped and floating
they come around
the bend of
  the river

dog masks

dreaming in the green water.

2

In the long grey days
of childhood
  they appeared
talked about in poultry stores
on saturday

or sometimes
in the country
with no one around ·for miles
they would be there
drying
threaded on fences

their teeth
their tangled smiles
waving in the grass.

FOUR APPEARANCES OF JOHN'S RED ROOSTER

1   John's red rooster off in the distance
      a peppery dance of rage

      White goats dreaming in clover
      he walks among them
      the only true critic
      in the entire landscape.

2   A choleric bonfire
      crossing the lawn

      in his crooked charge
      one murder red eye cocked up
      homing in on the shanks

      of poets and farmers alike.
      HOly Christ   the earth is
      awake when he leaps!

3   John's Red Rooster Running Away:
      with what purity of indignation
      he trundled off

      a boot in the asshole time and again.
      Adios into the falling sun

      angry wattles
      and an evening
      of sullen thought behind the evergreens.

4   Toward morning he crossed
     lines with a coyote

     we found russet feathers blowing
     across the morning snow
     two yellow legs alone in the frozen creekbank

     as if he had danced away
     into the earth.

THE OX

Under white sheets
I am a huge ox carcass
blue gristle
and purple red meat numb
in the deepness of the bed.
All buttocks and ballocks
I feel the heat of my fibers
seeping through the mattress.
Ragged winter

flies drone on the windowsill
and watch my great
cow lashes rise and fall.
The snowy hills outside
albino cattle
moving in the night
close in

and on the stairs
a butcher coughs
and rings his
meathooks like a bell.

BEAR/WOMAN

for Elaine Gill

All there is to
being a bear is you
  with your massive head
and eyes that seem to
know what the forest means
when it ceases to move

            you move
and it is with the heavy grace
of bears that
walk in the sky.

And now that I have found you
even the bears of
my dreams have stopped
showing their teeth

these last few nights.
They tell me I have gone beyond
that circle of fear,
they ride in
the back of pickup trucks
waving sticks tipped with flowers

and smiling a smile
that passes all wisdom.

GOPHERS AND MOLES OF AMERICA

We have the news for america
written on the gophers narrow teeth
on the blazing
starry nose of the mole.
The Gophers and Moles of America
cross the continent

looking for the open
sky in the middle of the earth.

Opening their hallways in the dark
they pass the ribs of red
woods and Indians.
They enter our coffin fields
bumping and turning

to emerge at night
beside our sleeping heads
with all the news.

The Dead Of America
Are Still Dying.
The Living
Stare Into The Earth.

The gophers and moles of america
tunnel their way to the stars.

THE MOSQUITO

Alone in the wet night
my blood is black and tingling
and I see
the mosquito on my forearm
like a bristling

mechanical lion

flown across
hundreds of landscapes
to find me just before dawn
standing strangely calm beside
the opening peony bush

It is a ceremony
as he prepares the moment
for our touch

his purring energy
draws pictures
in the air

his eyes are amber lights

that peer into my blood.

SKUNK HEAVEN

Skunks invaded all the town this summer
ruby eyed beside the garbage cans
or discovered by dogs as they
investigated lawns

they always came to face
sullen and confused
the pistol of deputy Charlie Rhodes

who was quoted while salting his
afternoon beer
on the question of what he did
with all those skunks:

    "I send them to skunk heaven."

Dreamily returning home that night
pissed to the gills
the firmament a massive streak
of black and white   he falls
asleep beside the road
and feels dreamy rabid teeth
against his skin

and Deputy Rhodes appears in skunk heaven
luminous stripes and black sheen
the foolish smiles
of skunks knocked on the head
tails half lifted;
skunks of all ages and persuasions
relaxing and drinking a musky beer
a red hole between each set
of rounded ears.

"Come over here" they are saying
"and show us your true stripe."

THE CATTLE

Night covers
the black angus herd

among dark cottonwoods
it shimmers against them
Insects weave
shivering cries
at their legs

far off
they smell dawn approaching

a pale glacier of light

their eyes luster unfolds
night seeps
into
their skin

THE MAN WHO SPOKE TO BOAT-TAILED GRACKLES

Fields By The River   that was
his first memory

and the boat-tailed grackles
gliding down the wind
tails half turned

settling in
to the fallen corn.

They surfaced in summer
long legged on the
new grass   and in conversation
each eye answered

a brilliant white ring
in the glossy blue black
green   and purple heads.

One day he found
the last word of his life
lying in the bottom of his skull

like the last dark
apple in a barrel.

And when he had nothing
more to say   he had

grackles in the spring sky
talking and flying.

WOLF

Full fire of that which
only glows in dogs
let him be   the only
moving thing along the timberline

his eyes cold suns
in the mountain whiteness.
At night: dark maps
of entrails on the snow.

There is no hero hidden
in the plume of his breath

although men pack together and declare
themselves wolves   lone wolves
werewolves. Six million boy scouts
follow Akela to their doom
his face pinned to their hearts.

There is no man inside his skin.

He is
his own brother.

GORILLA TALISMAN

for elaine

1.

All those days alone
in grandmas big white house on the prairie
she did not fear the coyotes
tornados or bitter dakota dust

not even the gut-chewing Indians
who wandered by without a word
got under her skin. No   it was

something else   far out in the
shimmering heat she always thought she saw
a gorilla riding up the trail.

Each day he appeared at the foot of the sky
a big hairy hombre
astride a spindly horse
and when the sun went down
he would still be burning up the horizon.

At night   she said
she even heard him out there
woofing and grumbling to himself
far off beneath the stars.

2.

Dad suffered from Depression Gorillas
after his hundred dollar paychecks.
Leaving grocery stores with his
order book   he would suddenly see

a gorilla in a cloth cap
lounging on the corner.
Gorillas chewing toothpicks
would follow him out of cafes
deftly freezing up his half-digested meals.

He began to find his samples pawed over
a trail of coarse gorilla hairs
leading away from the car
and in hotel rooms
dreams bubbled up
of super salesmen gorillas
taking away his territory.

The last gorilla he saw
he remembers clearly   sat elbow to elbow
with him   drinking coffee in a small cafe
and reached a massive hand over
to palm the customary nickel tip.

When the Depression ended they faded
and left him with a bad stomach
delicate nerve ends
a fear of hairy men.

3.

It was the night of the
Fancy Dress Ball
to which in my seventh year
I escorted a seven year old raving
breastless beauty. Suddenly
a gorilla swung upon the scene
fangs foremost via the
cut glass chandelier.
My classmates went crazy
while I calmly stashed my young virgin
and sent out a call for everyones
forks and knives.

My weaponry spread before me
I began hurling them at the oncoming
gorilla. Soon the dining rooms
quality sterling began to take its toll.
The gorilla gave one final clanking
step and expired three feet from
the table   resembling
a giant silver brooch.

Night after night
I awoke to it
heavy with the imprint of that repeated death
the gorillas leering grin
intricate vines and leaves
worked on the silver handles

and the joy that leaped beneath
my cummerbund
as each crazy fork struck home.

4.

My daughters total love goes out
unasked to howlers   chimpanzees
the whooping gibbon.
Even the mandrills horror
is redeemed by his azure cheeks

but the deal is off
when a gorilla comes on the scene.

I show her
pictures of the villain
mumbling shyly through the leaves
a strand of exotic spinach
hanging from his lips.
The gorilla is quiet.   The gorilla
minds his own business.

But there is something
I don't know: the gorilla
lives in the closet
waits to leap from the refrigerator
brushes his teeth silently in the bathroom.
Five hundred gorillas are shuffling
outside the front door.
Gorillas are driving the buses
leaping through the supermarket cereal.
A gorilla is picking his teeth.
A gorilla is peeling an orange.

Somewhere on the prairie
a gorilla is trimming his toenails
around the campfire.
Gorillas are sleeping it off in Hoboken
and a rampant gorilla is bulldozed
into the city dump with 500 pounds
of clanking silverware.

A gorilla is reading this poem.
His finger moves
slowly along the page.
Now he is thinking

All mercy to the gorilla of life
all peace to the gorilla of poetry.
Let them be

glorious in
the beauty of their tribe.

ANTS

Each night
black ants cross
the blackness of my inner eyelids

with a calm precision

each of them carries a grain
of something important.
           Building a picture

which becomes my evening dream

and all night my body
will quietly hum in the dark
trying hard to photograph   preserve

the secret
for my morning eyes.

THE APPALOOSA COLT

four days old, that disappeared
one night,
we found at morning

only one thin foreleg
gently flexed in the sawgrass
like some cryptic artifact
the cream yellow hoof
shank   knee   and where
the body should have been,
a clean uncommon space.

Coyotes or mad farm dogs
had crossed the hill, their
scent posts made a square
target of the pasture

and I waited with a rifle
for their return all afternoon.
But coyotes dreamt beneath the earth
and farm dogs watched me
deep within their
distant yards.
I slept

and saw the skins of horses
move across the sun
like spotted clouds.

DOWNY WOODPECKER

White feathers   charcoal-barred
on the attic window a
three-pointed burst of feathers
where a bird laid his skull
against the glass
(clear stain radiating outward)

he's gone: fifteen feet
into the snowbank below.

With spring the rain-washed body
returns   flat whites and greys;
a clever drawing
worked into the grass

and like a memorial tonight
a sense of flight radiates the house.

ZOO TIGER

The tiger has hepatitis.
He comes before us
to plead his case. We watch
his breath   pale green
in the concrete room.

The great square head
speaks intelligently
point by point
 ("remember that I do not
  even have the memory
  of walking in tall grass")

He is old
and very concerned

but a certain flair is lacking
in the monotonous stripes
and the tigerish orange has gone
like old velvet   ("please
   consider also
   I have not complained
   unfairly. .")

We look ahead
on our mimeo sheets.
   The Ring-Tailed Cat
   has rickets
and looks more spirited.
In an adjacent cage he
nervously rehearses.

The tigers eyes are growing deep.
He coughs into the silence

and stares above our heads.

CARDINALS

The room has filled with cardinals
glowing in the dark
like scarlet flames   they wait
upon the dresser, bed
and window ledge
    poised omens

opening the room
with fierce red light.

What they are
messengers of
it is not known.
They give no sign   they only
watch where I lie
sleepless

expecting
any moment
        their strange
and beautiful voice.

THE DEER

We have found each other
frozen still   our faces held up to the air

(a red deer silent in the red-orange woods)

There is something he expects of me
although my hands are empty.

His eyes swirl oily colors
shining inward
and light grows
from his nostrils and ears.

There is something
I desire of him.
It seems very important

but the words leave my mouth
in a colorless stream
and where they sink into his neck
a new red hair appears.
His antlers branch like bone white trees

above the yellow oak and maple.
He grows   turning back
hooves drawing up from the hills all around
as he leaps into the hard
black sky

and pulls me out
of my self like an arrow.

RACCOONS

This morning the highway
is full of their bodies
    paws curled in
  to a final leap
and face masks
knocked awry

they lay fatly on the gravel
      like old bums
  guard hairs rippling
in the wake of passing cars

as if   on this most
beautiful of days
they are only dreaming
    of evening   and rivers

and trees   that rise forever.

JUMPING SPIDER IN THE CENTER

for Pat

The first jumping spider of spring
Phidippus audax
black and orange on the
tip of a pink hyacinth

eyes cluttered with rainbows
colliding in the april light

If I'm awake
never let me sleep

Above and to the right
the full blown apricot tree
is swirling with bees

O babe   if I'm sleeping
I hope you are too.

THE OLD DOG

I opened a room in my head
and there was the old dog
I'd grown with   waiting
beside a blue divan.

We embraced solemnly
the familiar phosphorous smell of his breath
and shoulder blades like smooth hard wings
slanting under my hands.

"A long trip. . ." he said
politely looking away
". . .it seemed like a hundred miles"
and silence covered
his silky spotted coat.

On the wall a movie was showing
of our last encounter
a final ride to the vets
his heart grown soft in age
the useless back legs stiff with fear.
When I lifted him
from the pickup seat

he'd pissed all over himself
and the brown eyes
lost all intelligence.

Ten years it took
to fly from death to dreams
a hundred abstract miles.
Little narrow teeth of his lower jaw
flickering in the light

the old dog watched the movie
like a perfect gentleman
pretending it was the story
of someone elses life.

ALL PIGS

One night
we were all pigs.
You were a pig with a wrinkled nose.
I was a pig with starry eyes.

We had garbanzos and porkchops for supper
and laughed hysterically
our tiny hooves knocking in glee.
Suddenly there was a knock on the door.

It was the neighborhood delegation
hairy pigs   feathered pigs   horned pigs
pigs with gleaming smiles
and bouffant hairdos.
We all had something to drink.

On the television a group of pigs
on horseback caught a renegade pig
"Somebody get a rope," said
an old pig with whiskers.

It was so much
fun when we were all pigs.
I remember it well.
Lovely pink
strangers moved among us.

You were the pig with starry eyes
and I was the pig with beautiful teeth.

THE BADGER

dog bear
of the grass

Striped hair
jeweled with morning water,
he speaks
with one foot
in the circle of iron

thin black lips rippling over teeth

and offers a trade:
the metal trap
for the ground on which
it lies.
But I see myself clearly

raising the rifle.
My hands are freezing
and his foot is a burst of cold bone

that claws at my eyes.

THE BLUE-EYED PELICAN

for Jose

The pelicans all safely tucked away
in corners of the city
we walk the narrow avenue
down to the sea at night

my brother-in-laws sleek head
like the darkest of sea birds
moving to the waters voice.
Far to our right the port of Callao
wrinkles the ocean with light

and his little girls
hang on my arms
quick as fish in the heavy air.
I am the strange foreign uncle
who can make two pesetas
leap into three between his fingertips.
It is what I have always

wanted to be
the last prodigal piece
of an aching oceanic dream

a solemn blue-eyed pelican
finding my place in the dark.

THE PANDA

What can he want
appearing suddenly in my night life
   with those melancholy
   black stained eyes
   and shoe peg teeth?
War with China?
A misspent childhood?

The action goes on without him
as I ravage wet-mouthed starlets
and insult men twice my size
yet he remains
   seated in a corner of the dream
   like a forlorn trademark
   fumbling with a bamboo shoot.

It is only afterward
when I stand triumphant
and self-important over the
wrecked images
   that I turn to him

   and realize at last
that the face of my wife

when lost in her own dreams

assumes that same expression
which is at once
both comic
and full of unspeakable grief.

WHALES

The quality of sleep in bathtubs
sinks the body deeper
with each breath

water darkens the cold porcelain
receding into a distant shore
and the sun fades out forever

above the deepening layers of light.
The buzz of someones power mower
has become a creaking
of massive fields of water.

Now you are
down among the whales
as they pass   their squeaking
banshee songs swell
beneath the green black sea.

They move along
the seabed like dark hills
and in the nearest throat

in that dark and private space
your body   quietly rides

fingers   rising and   falling
in the   flow   of his breath.

BUTTERFLIES & COYOTE

We are driving through
the butterflies of the world
all at once

five miles out of Tipton Kansas
they appear across the
purple clover tops
like a floating memory

Yellow Alfalfas   Viceroys
Mourning Cloaks and Monarchs
do their crazy jig along the highway

flashing off to answer
the call of lonely dreamers everywhere.

And as if we had
a choice of dreams
a distant coyote runs in the opposite field

smiling head rising and falling
in the green wheat sea.

CHICKENS

Six chickens at a time
when company came

and these bled right.
Not the awkward body searching
for its severed head

but tied up gently on the
clothesline   blue-grey feet
against the sky;
one razor stroke
across each throat.

Gentle Mr. Jensen
who could tell your chickens
would be with me all these years?
But those fanned out wings
have opened many nights
for no good cause.

I need only to hear
the word "dumbly"
and twelve slowly blinking eyelids
fill my head

or driving in the countryside
I see far off
a tiny clothesline
bits of laundry shining in the sun

and suddenly the pale sheets
are draining breath

bright stars of blood
beneath them on the grass.

GRASSHOPPER REVENGE

Grasshoppers:
I have a statement.

You strong yellow ones
of the intricate mouths
and brown arrow legs

you dusty
toadlike ones

and the narrow-shouldered
green with long neurotic faces

Gentlemen:
I surrender.
Your orange
chinese paper wings have over
taken me at last
and your polyhedral eyes
stare accusations into mine.

Each night for twenty years I've found
your eggs inside my underwear
each dawn I sniff your
umber spittle on my hands.

And now for what it's worth
I confess to various deaths in
sunflower fields (I was the
master of homicide; your jointed legs
and telescopic bellies I knew all
the weak spots). But those days
are gone forever

and we have both
grown wise beyond our years.

You see my eyes
how big with guilt they are. My mouth
works nervously in four directions
and my screams have soured the milk of all
young mothers in the neighborhood.

Yet I have had nothing to do
with your kind for fifteen years

with the exception of eating one of you
fried as a party diversion.
Surely that was a forgivable crime gentlemen.

So I say to you today:
let us now desist.
Begin your long journey back through the snows
and turn your vengeance
back upon the plains.

When I walk in
fields humming with your bodies
we will meet each other lightly

we will pass
like old and graceful enemies.

AMERICAN LION

Long limbed walker on the canyon rim
thicket screamer

we crawl off into dreams
of cougar catamount panther puma
cushion footed dreamer

> sandy traveler who carries
> the souls of dead men
> between his shoulderblades
> clouds in his teeth

on the sole of each foot
a map of the stars

and the lions dream crosses ours
the cougar has entered the city
dining on twice-removed meat
selling cars to video grey faces
so recently hated and feared

In the cottonwoods
murmuring by the river
in the grainy heart of boulders
on moonlit slopes
lie down for a continent of skins
scattered claws that once spoke
their simple name so well

In the dark green pines
and across the neck of the running deer
lie down in grief
for the lion in the necktie.

MANTIS LADIES

My brain kicked over
like an earth bound stone
four Chinese Mantids
standing upright on the furrows

green triangular heads of elegant ladies
and pinpoint of brown light
in the depths of each eye

"The Curious Asexual Stare
of The Praying Mantis
is The Essence of Asexual Curiosity"
says the slowly
turning stone

four Chinese Ladies
nibble my fingers

"I'm only here for sex" I say
suddenly ashamed of their
beauty: green clothes
green rosebush   green roses

green ankles surrounding
the cold grey stone.

THE GREAT NEVADA MOUSE PLAGUE

It was in the great Nevada mouse plague
of nineteen o seven
the mice were like grey daisies
mincing through the desert.
Praise the mice.

The mice came
and so the hawks and owls came
and the foxes and coyotes and snakes.
Everybody showed up.
It was a great time for animals.

The mice took over
all the buildings all the beds
eyes bulging like currants.
Mice in the toes of boots
mice in the mailbox

mice in the pickle barrels
praise the mice
a dreamy mantle of mice
too heavy to lift
falling over the state.

They died face down
in the sweet milk pails.
They were crushed between
the bodies of lovers
and their hearts exploded
on the courthouse lawn.
Praise the mice.

The delicate scribble of mice
became a constant
background hum
fading away at last
crossing the borders at night.
O praise the mice
they left a mouse
in every memory
a mouse in every brain.

Praise the mice.
What a great joke on Nevada
in nineteen o seven.

HAWK TOTEMS

All along the highway
hawks are down out of the fog

dark heart bodies on fence poles
and the solitary osage orange

their clear and terrible eyes
hooked over shoulders a gaze

that pierces the private sleep
of early travelers

like a dream swelling
out of this foggy winter morning

'two below in tupelo'
moaning on the radio

and even the pill-heavy truckdrivers
whooping in joy
at wild hawks.

SEAGULL DREAM

I saw a seagull
pierced by knives

I saw hands
white as the ocean sky
on every face

I saw a seagull screaming
from a herons mouth

I saw the encampments of man
blaze white with fear

I saw a seagull
burning with a bone white face

white eyes   white fire
a narrow skull
that spoke all names.

MORNING CROW

The one true
heart of black
in that city landscape

    Just at dawn
he appears
      a large black flake
drifting over the buildings
          silently

    leaving the city
where   all night
he has starred

in the midnight dreams
of higher animals.

OUR LIFE DISGUISED AS BUTTERFLIES

The first few hours of our lives
were a Pink-Edged Sulphur.
Our eyes opened we began
swimming through the air.

We called the sun Sleepy Orange.
We called the sky Crowberry Blue.
We lay down and slept
in the heaps of dead leaves.

The Malicious Skipper   The
Swarthy Skipper and
Duke's Skipper arrived in pin
stripe suits and limousines
offering women and money.
We shot and buried them
in the western glow before supper.

Red Admiral   White Admiral:
men with colorful chests
congratulated us on the
arrival of pubic hair.

When we slept
our brain assumed its real name.
It was a Dreamy Dusky Wing
afloat in the skull.

We named our marriage
Pearl Crescent after the
shapes and textures of love.

THE ANIMALS WE NEVER KNOW

The animals we never know
linger on the hazy margins

uncharted hair and horn
fur feathers and scales
sliding into position
at the corner of our eyes

always just
disappearing through the trees
fading back into adjacent
darkened rooms
their bodies vibrate
with knowledge of us.

Our wings have fallen off.
Our hearts begin to
smoke with useless energy
we grow like pale swamp flowers
brains swollen with mud.

The animals we never know
drift in the shadows
they lick our sleeping skin
and tangle in the falling breath.

Dreams of our foolish journey
fill their eyes like snow.